No Bullying Starts Today

Awareness Raising Days on Bullying

by

George Robinson
Jane Sleigh
Barbara Maines

© George Robinson, Jane Sleigh, Barbara Maines 1995

Apart from any fair dealing for the purposes of research or
private study, or criticism or review, as permitted under the
Copyright, Designs and Patents Act, 1988, this publication may be
reproduced, stored or transmitted in any form, or by any means,
only with the prior permission in writing of the publishers, or in
the case of reprographic reproduction, in accordance with the terms of
licences issued by the Copyright Licensing Agency. Enquiries concerning
reproduction outside those terms should be sent to the publishers.

Rights to copy pages marked as handouts, certificates or overhead foils are
extended to the purchaser of the publication for his/her use.

The right of the author to be identified as Author of his work has been asserted
by him/her in accordance with the Copyright, Design and Patents Act 1988.

SAGE Publications Ltd
1 Oliver's Yard
55 City Road
London EC1Y 1SP

SAGE Publications Inc
2455 Teller Road
Thousand Oaks
California 91320

SAGE Publications India Pvt. Ltd
B 1/I 1 Mohan Cooperative Industrial Area
Mathura Road, New Delhi 110 044
India

SAGE Publications Asia-Pacific Pte Ltd
33 Pekin Street #02-01
Far East Square
Singapore 048763

www.luckyduck.co.uk

Library of Congress Control Number Available

British Library Cataloguing in Publication Data
A catalogue record for this book is available from the British Library

ISBN 978-1-87394-201-7

Staff Guidelines
to help you organise and present your own Special Day

The first important book on bullying was published in this country in 1989. [Besag, V.] By 1992 the subject was constantly featured in newspaper articles and on television programmes. Parents and teachers were talking about bullying as a frequent and serious problem in schools. Our first anti-bullying initiative was a response to one school's request for help following a suicide attempt by a teenage girl pupil. We encouraged the staff in planning a tutorial programme of social and friendship skills but we all agreed that the seriousness of the incident warranted a high profile and significant event which would demonstrate to the whole community that this school took its responsibility for anti-bullying work seriously. On December 14th 1990 a team of facilitators ran a whole day of activities for years eight and nine in this one school. The day was filmed and the published video and book record our first work on bullying in schools. [Maines and Robinson 1991.]

Since then many similar days have taken place with countless variations on the original programme. This publication gathers together the experience of those who planned and ran the days. The collection of ideas is intended to help you prepare and run your own awareness raising day for pupils. Some of the content has been written up as the action plans developed and was not originally intended for publication. We have not edited these notes.

Several models, activities, ideas and worksheets are included. We hope that these will provide ideas and resources to build upon. All parts of the book can be photo-copied for use in your own school.

You may find the video Stamp out Bullying a good starting point for staff who intend to organise the day. It has been described as "a warts and all" account, but it provides a vivid record of one special day.

There are certain principles that we think are essential ingredients of any day.

Make it Special

If you want the pupils to remember the day, you have to make it memorable.

* Make it a non-uniform day.
* Provide refreshments, soft drinks, doughnuts, hamburgers. Local business might support you.
* Give it high-profile. Involve the local media, TV, radio, press might be interested. Stress you don't have an exceptional problem with bullying. **All** schools have problems with bullying. This school is going to tackle it.
* Involve as many people as possible, not just to attend, but to be active participants. The day has many group activities, these could be run not just by teaching staff, but by:

>   Education Welfare Officers   Governors
>   Social Workers   Non-teaching Assistants
>   Parents   Older Pupils
>   Educational Psychologists   School Meals Supervisors
>   School Nurse   School Secretary
>   Community Police   School Technicians

Remember, learning is not just for pupils. What better way to learn than to be active, involved participants.

Planning

Because the days give teachers and other facilitators the opportunity to use their own strengths and talents, the planning seems to work well when one, or a small team takes overall responsibility for the whole day and then delegates activities and responsibilities to team members, many of whom will make surprising and innovative contributions.

Most of the work takes place before the day and the better prepared the team, the better the day will run. The example in Appendix 1 illustrates the way one school worked to prepare before the event.

A balanced programme might have:

1. An initial introduction on bullying for all participants
2. Activities carried out in smaller groups
3. A final closing for all participants

There are other decisions to be taken:

Who are the participants?
Which year groups will be involved, some schools make this a special event for Year 7. Others make it a much larger event, involving more than one year group, some schools make it a whole school event.

Who will make up the team of facilitators?
School organisation, enthusiasm and availability of colleagues outside school should all be taken into account.

What is to be the content?
A range of activities provides variety and maintains interest for the young people and the adults. Whilst some facilitators might be encouraged to try something new – nobody should be left feeling unsure or uncomfortable. It is better to drop an activity, however good, than to run it without confidence.

Refreshments, breaks and lunch
Special food and drink can give a real "lift" to the whole day. Local firms might sponsor the school with a contribution, doughnuts and pizzas are very popular.

Media coverage
This group could prepare a press release or encourage radio or TV interest. If you make it easy for the media you are more likely to get coverage.

Resourcing the School
It is vital that a small team organises rooms, prepares for different activities, making sure videos, worksheets, instruction sheets for group leaders are available.

Organising the Groups
You need to consider the composition and functions of the groups.
* If your event is across age groups, we suggest you have mixed age groups
* Will you organise group leaders?
* First decide on the range of activities planned for the groups and then ask for volunteers to lead the groups. The more people you involve, the smaller the

groups will be. You may be surprised by some of the choices: you'll find art teachers who lead drama groups and drama teachers who lead music groups. Make a clear plan so pupils and staff know the composition of groups, location and time.

Involving Senior Management

The format of the day might have implications for

      room allocation   the timetable
      transport   meal arrangements

Senior management must be involved and approve all arrangements.

Informing the Parents

You need to inform parents. Decide what they need to know?
Would a letter be helpful informing them of both the purpose of the day and content? (see appendix 2 for an example).

Informing the Pupils

- How will you prepare the young people for the day?
- Will information be written or verbal?
- Will a programme be available in advance?

The same care should be taken in planning a day for pupils as would be expected by teachers for an Inset day.

Activities Before the Day

It may be helpful to start discussing with staff and governors the purpose of the day. To justify the need for every school to do something about bullying you could use the research findings from the DfE. funded project in Sheffield reported in the publication, "Don't Suffer in Silence" (1994).

Primary Schools
- 27% of young people report being bullied at least some time in the term.
- 10% as often as once a week.

Secondary Schools
- 10% of young people report being bullied at least some time in the term.
- 4% as often as once a week.

50% of young people never report what is happening.

You may find it useful to find out about the pupils' perceptions by using a questionnaire (see appendix 3). It is important to make clear to both staff and pupils that the purpose of these activities is to establish a need for change.

Before the day you might find it useful to discuss the issue in staff meetings, perhaps using some activities to widen perceptions.

Evaluation

You may find it useful to evaluate the day from the perspective of the students and the group leaders. This will provide feedback that could:

* inform governors of the outcome of the day
* inform parents about how the pupils felt about the day
* help you improve future days

We did this in 1994 in one secondary school. It was apparent that the vast majority of the students found it a valuable experience. 70% of the students reported that the day was excellent or good (see appendix 4).

Whole School Policies

We believe that all schools must tackle bullying at two levels.

1. Prevention

This is achieved by creating a school ethos/atmosphere where all members of the community recognise bullying occurs but are committed to developing a community where the incidents of bullying will be reduced. A plan for prevention might include:

* Awareness raising days (as described in this publication)
* Curriculum strategies in subject areas such as English and P.S.E.
* Modelling good practice
* School Assemblies
* Producing poster weeks, where pupils produce posters on bullying issues
  ...and all the other wonderful ideas you will generate.

But....

No matter how good your preventative work is, bullying will still occur. Results from Sheffield and Norway suggest you can reduce bullying by 25% - 50% by whole school preventative approaches. This still leaves you with the need to have responses that will deal with bullying when it occurs. When schools implement good preventive work they will achieve a safer environment - there will be fewer incidents of bullying but it will also feel safer to talk about bullying **so there may actually be an increase in the number of incidents reported.**

2 Reacting to Bullying

There are various ideas about how to deal effectively with bullying. This publication is not intended to <u>deal with this issue.</u> For further information see "Don't Suffer in Silence" DfE. 1994 pages 48 - 57.

We recommend the **No Blame Approach** for dealing with bullying, but whatever your position, all schools need to remember bullying happens in all schools and it is essential to have a clear policy. Schools might find the publications by Robinson and Maines (1994) helpful in producing a policy.

The Format of Awareness Raising Days

Decide on your aims for the day: These might include:

1. to agree that bullying happens
2. to agree that bullying is damaging to the person that receives it
3. to agree that bullies are not nasty people and may not be fully aware of how their behaviour damages other people
4. to extend the definition of bullying to a wider range of behaviours
5. to learn something about group process
6. to experience group work
7. to provide opportunities through creative work for young people to express feelings about bullying
8. to provide empowering opportunities for problem solving "what can we do", "what will we do"
9. to celebrate the work done on the day
10. to prepare for further work to be done in the future

You can add or delete as necessary, but it is important to clearly identify your specific aims.

Organising the Day

The Start - preparing the pupils for the whole day. This is the crucial part. You need to capture their interest, touch their hearts and open their minds for a change in attitude.

The Middle Bits - this is where the learning will occur. You need to provide a variety of learning experiences. It is suggested that we have a preferred channel of learning. Some of us are visual learners, some auditory learners and some kinaesthetic learners. Teachers all know that sitting and listening for long periods of time is hard work, so the middle bits should be varied and interactive.

The End - there should be a distinct ending to the event. This helps celebrate what has happened, helps draw together what you hope the pupils have learned and prepares the ground for future work. The pupils should leave the day feeling it has been a positive experience and excited about what they can do in the future in a school that recognises bullying does occur but feels confident that it knows how to deal with it. The underlying message should include the important point that there is nothing different about bullies and victims. Anybody can be a victim and lots of very nice young people can sometimes bully.

The days have been organised in two alternative formats. Both start and end with all the pupils together in one forum. There are two different models for the middle sections of the day.

In the first model each facilitator runs the full programme of morning activities with one group of pupils. In the second, the facilitator repeats an activity and the young people move from one facilitator to the next in order to pick up the full programme.

MODEL A
All the pupils do the same morning activities at the same time. In the afternoon they choose from a menu of activities.

Suggested timetable

9.00 - 9.30	Introduction - everyone together
9.35 - 10.35	Session one - in small groups
10.45 - 11.05	Break
11.10 - 12.20	Session two - in small groups
12.20 - 1.30	Lunch
1.30 - 2.45	Choice of workshops
2.50 - 3.30	Closing session - everyone together

MODEL B
A variety of activities are arranged with each pupil doing the same activities during the day but at different times. In one school we had 45 groups rotating through nine parallel sessions of five different activities.

Suggested timetable

9.00 - 9.45	Introduction - everyone together
9.50 - 10.35	Session one - in small groups
10.35 - 10.50	Break
10.55 - 11.40	Session two - in small groups
11.45 - 12.30	Session three - in small groups
12.30 - 1.10	Lunch
1.15 - 2.00	Session four - small groups
2.05 - 2.50	Session five - small groups
2.55 - 3.20	Closing session - everyone together

The First Session
All young people together

We have run the first session in a variety of ways. The day should begin with activities which have high impact and capture attention. However, whilst it may be acceptable to allow the young people to experience strong feelings, it is also important that they should feel safe. Personal experiences and exposure to risk should not be included at the start of the session but later in small and more secure group settings. Below are some suitable starter activities. Some of these are supported by overhead transparencies printed up in appendix 5 - indicated in the text with the symbol Ξ.

1 Introduce the aims of the day Ξ
The list of aims can be presented on a handout or projected as an overhead visual aid for discussion.

2 Bullying is serious
The statistics about the frequency of bullying in British schools or data from a school survey can establish the extent of the problem and an agreement to go ahead and improve things.

3 Victims are very vulnerable
This is a quotation from a journal called Japan Quarterly. It is called "Victims have no friends".

> Before taking his life, the boy wrote a message in the class diary, a portion of which I quote.
>
> *"I decided to kill myself because day after day I go to school and only bad things happen. Nothing good ever happens to me. If the kids in my class could be in my shoes they would understand how I feel. If only they knew how I feel every day. Even in my dreams there are nothing but bad things. The only one I can talk to is the hamster, but the hamster can't speak back. Maybe my being born was a mistake... I can't stop the tears now. There was one, only one thing I wanted while I was alive, a friend I could talk to, really talk to from the heart. Just one friend like that, only one, was all I wanted."*

Ξ.

4 What is Bullying? - Agreeing a definition.
Get the pupils to discuss in pairs a definition of bullying.
Take some feedback. Make the following points:
* It is not just physical harm.
* It happens over a period of time.
* Sometimes it is very hard to notice; a look can terrify.

[see page 15 for a possible definition].

5 Scenarios
Get a group of staff to act out some bullying scenarios [these need to be rehearsed and not over acted. They are not intended to be funny!]
* Teasing   * Exclusion, being left out   * Name calling
* Extortion, taking crisps, sweets   * Threatening aggression
* Physical aggression, pushing, shoving.

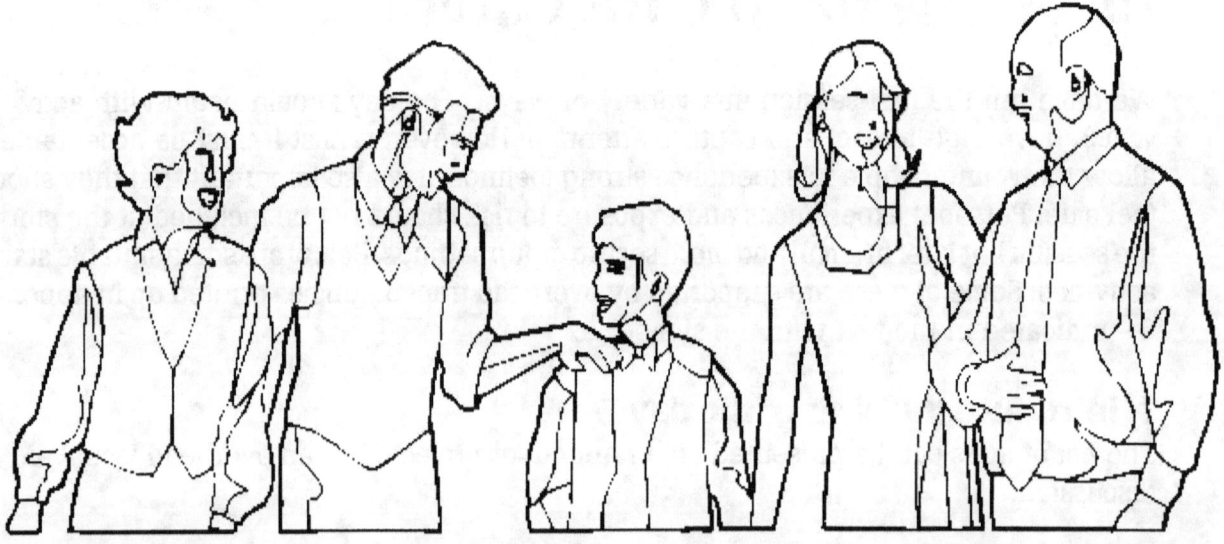

6 Mild and Serious Bullying

Ask the pupils to discuss in 2/3s which was the most severe and how it make them feel. Take feedback. Make the point:

The seriousness of bullying can only be judged by the person who is hurting. Sometimes physical hurt can be less painful than relentless teasing.

7 Different people react in different ways Ξ

Choose two teachers who wear glasses. Ask the group to imagine that the two members of staff are Year 7 pupils who sit together in class. Use the teachers' first names. If you wear glasses, make yourself the victim.

All the kids in the class think it's fun to call Mary and Tom names because they wear glasses. They call them Speccies, Four Eyes, Cow and Gate, Goggle Eyes etc.

It has no effect on Tom, he feels good in his glasses, he has designer frames and everybody in his family wears glasses. He laughs it off.

For Mary, it is different. The family is short of money and she couldn't get the fashionable designer frame glasses she wanted. She got the cheapest frames in the shop. Nobody else in her family wears glasses, she pretends she doesn't care, but deep down she's desperate for the name calling to stop. It's killing her!

8 Who is Involved?

Explain that if you know bullying is happening and you do nothing, then you are involved. There is no such thing as a bystander or an observer. You can either do something to stop it, or choose to do nothing to make it better.

    But why don't victims tell?
    Why do the people who see it happen keep quiet.
    Discuss in 2/3s

Take feedback and make the point:
Many young people are frightened that if they tell, somehow it will become worse. After today we hope each one of you will know what to do to make it better.

9 Expecting the Victim to help him/herself

People often say:
    Ignore it   Fight back
    Call them names   Stand up for yourself

11

If the victim could do this s/he would. If the victim tries to follow this advice and it doesn't work, it makes him/her think "It is my fault. There is something wrong with me."

Read this quotation to the pupils:

*"You have to learn to stand up for yourself!" says my mother.
"Don't let them push you around.
Don't be spineless.
You have to have more backbone."*

I think of sardines and their backbones. You can eat their backbones. The bones crumble between your teeth in one touch and they fall apart. This must be what my own backbone is like; hardly there at all. What is happening to me is my own fault, for not having more backbone.

Ξ CATS EYE by Margaret Attwood (1990).

10 Being Different

Bullying usually means somebody is picked on for being different. But who decides what is different?

In 2/3s ask the young people to think of a time when they have been discriminated against, have been left out, or when they discriminated against someone else. After a few minutes' discussion take some feedback

Ask for a show of hands: "Put your hand up if you are not different!" Read the quotation below or hand it out as a take-home. Ξ

Jack Straw, the MP wrote this which clearly describes how a group of children decided to pick on somebody who they made different.

It wasn't classical bullying. There was no single big lad beating up a smaller one. Indeed very little of the bullying was physical at all. It was verbal, psychological, insidious and, in many ways the worse for that. Paul had been chosen as the odd one out. I have no idea how the rest of us made that choice. Certainly it was never a conscious decision. But the rest of us - each of whom, I guess, also found the frugal atmosphere of a Fifties boarding school quite hard to bear - picked on Paul. He smelt - but didn't we all with only one bath and one clean shirt a week, who wouldn't? He was stupid - though his academic results were the same as the rest of us. He didn't join in. We made sure of that. Above all he was different. I can't for the life of me remember why, or how, except that we had to make him different and we did.

Jack Straw - Daily Mirror. January 18th 1995

We are all different. Maybe it's better if we used words like "special" or "unique".

End the First session with a powerful message to all the young people that they can take positive action to stop bullying. Each one of them can be the person who makes a real difference. Explain that when someone is upset or hurting a little bit of kindness can make all the difference.

Working in small groups

After the opening session the young people will work in small groups, ten to twenty. The composition of the groups requires thought and careful planning. Decide whether to arrange a mix from year groups or tutor groups, and whether some young people should be together with or separated from particular peers.

Lists of group members and room allocations must be clearly communicated so that the young people can move quickly to the next place of work. Some schools use older pupils to act as guides. Rooms should be clearly marked with a list of group members posted on the door.

During group work some young people are involved in strong emotional reactions. Usually this can be managed within the group but it is important to have a member of staff free to spend time with any young person who is upset.

Plan for Model A
Everyone does the same activity at the same time.

First Session - Group work, Circle time.
The room must be set out with chairs in a circle, one for each participant.
Resources: OHP/flip chart/board and markers / paper for students.

The activities can vary according to how well the group members know each other. Remind the students of the ground rules:

> **Listen to others**
> **No put downs**
> **The right to pass**

There are a variety of activities from which to choose a selection which suits the group. It is important that the facilitator feels comfortable with every activity. Some of the beginning activities encourage trust between the group members before the work progresses to affective work concerned with bullying.

Seated Circle
You need at least twenty students for this. Ask them to stand in a circle, right shoulders into the centre. Move towards the centre until students are close together. They then place their hands on the shoulders of the person in front. At a signal all the students sit on the knees of the person behind. If the group is working together they should be able to stay sitting and take their arms off the shoulders of the student in front!

Rocking in threes
Two students stand facing each other with another in between them. The two rockers stand at about a metre and a half apart. The person in the middle stands with feet together and is gently rocked between the two rockers. This requires trust of the people rocking them.

Working as a Team
The Human Machine: One volunteer stands in the centre of the circle and starts off an action and noise which could be made on a factory production line. Another student joins in and makes a complementary action and noise. Gradually everyone joins in. Each student should have contact with one of the previous participants.

The Human Knot
Choose one group member to stand outside the circle. This person will direct the activity later. Remaining students stand in a circle and face inwards. Everyone crosses hands and joins hands with any two people across the group. This makes a tangle of connected hands. When everyone is well linked, then ask the student outside the circle to give directions for untangling the web without breaking the linked hands.

These activities all encourage physical contact and break down inhibitions. If a student chooses not to join then allow this and later offer a responsibility - for example checking that no links have been broken in The Human Knot.

Changing Places
This activity allows the facilitator to move young people around and mix up friendship pairs if appropriate.
Students seated in a circle of chairs. Facilitator calls out, Change places..
* all those with brown shoes
* all those who like playing computer games
* all those who have a brother and a sister

From this activity the facilitator can introduce less neutral issues, particularly the knowledge of and the experience of bullying in school.

Silent Statements
By changing places young people can indicate a positive response without speaking. Change places...
* if you were worried about bullying when you came to the school
* if you have seen people being bullied at school
* if you think bullying happens in the playground
* if you think there is more than one type of bullying

Changing places can be used at any point in circle work when a mix up or repositioning would be helpful.

Statement Line

Another way of making a silent statement is to stand along a Statement Line. Explain that one end of the line is **strongly agree** and the opposite end is **strongly disagree** with a gradual change along the invisible line. Tell the students that they are not allowed to comment on where other people stand or to influence them in any way.

Make a statement and ask the students to stand along the line according to their feelings about the statement.

* bullying is a big problem in this school
* physical bullying is worse than name calling
* a lot of people are bullied but don't tell anyone
* being left out is a form of bullying.

When the students sit back down take some general comments about the way individuals distributed themselves along the line.

Clarification of terms

Go round the circle and ask each person to describe a type of bullying behaviour. Ask a scribe to record the responses.

The scribe could record them in groups according to the types such as physical, emotional, verbal ......

Discuss whether all forms of aggression are bullying. Ask the young people to indicate whether they agree or disagree that it is bullying if someone is: called a name, teased, excluded or hit once.

Give and display a definition of Bullying

There are many definitions of bullying but all have three things in common:

* it is deliberately hurtful behaviour
* it is repeated often over a period of time
* it is difficult for those being bullied to stop the process.

"A pupil is being bullied, or picked on, when another pupil or group of pupils say nasty things to him or her. It is also bullying when a pupil is hit, kicked, threatened, locked inside a room, sent nasty notes, when no-one ever talks to him or her and things like that.

These things can happen frequently and it is difficult for the pupil being bullied to defend himself or herself. It is also bullying when a pupil is teased repeatedly in a nasty way.

However, if two pupils of equal power or strength have an occasional fight or quarrel, this is not bullying."

[Bullying, Don't Suffer in Silence 1994 page 24].

Feelings and Effects of Bullying

Divide the young people into threes and ask them to talk about the feelings and effects of bullying on the victim, the bully and the watchers.
Each member of the group should remember the feelings for either the victim, bully or watcher.

Go round the circle and ask each person in turn to give a feeling for his or her category. These can be recorded.

My Rights

Divide the young people into groups of four. After talking about the effects of bullying on all involved, the rights of a child in a school can now be agreed.
Each group should record a list of student rights.

The list will generally include the right to be regarded with respect, safe from ridicule or "put down", the right to be different and the right to be accepted.
The facilitator should draw out this theme from the students contributions or by adding to them [see appendix 5].

The agreed list can be kept as a permanent record.

Celebrating Differences

As much bullying is the result of perceived differences we can address the issue by celebrating the fact that no two people are the same.
Why is it OK to be keen on football, basketball or other sport but not on mathematics or science?

Point out that any one "star" might be dependent upon others with different skills. A soccer player needs medical expertise to plan a training programme, media scientists to broadcast his performance. We are all dependent on the ways in which our different skills and interests contribute to society.
To establish the differences within the group
Change places...
- * if you are left handed
- * if you wear glasses or contact lenses
- * if one of your parents was born in a country other than England

Pair up the students around the circle and ask each one to find something special about his/her partner. Give some examples:

- * I am special because I was born in Scotland
- * I am special because I have had several ear operations and can now hear properly
- * I am special because my mum was born in Jamaica and my dad in Indonesia
- * I am special because I am very tall

To feed back to the group ask each student to say what is special about his/her partner.

Celebrate the fact that they are all special in some way.

Guided Recall
Ask students to sit comfortably with hands on laps and eyes shut.
Using a calm, steady voice, allowing time for each memory, define situations and ask them to remember how they felt when............

* You are watching someone being bullied, how does it make you feel? What do you want to do about it? Do you do anything about it? Why?

* You are being bullied or insulted by another person, remember what it felt like, what did they do or say to you, remember what you did or said.

* You bullied someone or were unpleasant to someone. How did you feel at the time? What did you do or say? How did you feel afterwards?

Feedback
Ask students if they are willing to discuss any of their experiences? If the facilitator starts to disclose an experience it may give the others the confidence to join in. The discussion should concentrate on the feelings of the victims and the bullies.

Endings
Check that group members feel they have achieved the aims of the session. Point out that if bullying is going to stop everyone must share a responsibility for this change.

Sentence Completion
Go around the circle asking for a sentence completion beginning
* The thing I will do to stop bullying is...

Choose a statement line to close the session
* the session has helped us to understand the effects of bullying.
* we will stop and think before we act in a way that could be hurtful to others.
* we know that it is important to tell someone if bullying is happening to us or someone we know.

Round
At the end of this session conduct a round. Ask all students individually to share something that they have learnt or found interesting during the sessions experienced so far. This enables the facilitator to gauge how much information has been assimilated and answer any questions that may be raised.

Thank each member of the group for his/her contribution.

Note: The mood of the group members and the depths to which they explore issues will determine the mix of activities which make up this session. The facilitator should not stick rigidly to pre-set timings or a fixed order but be willing to spend time on one activity or change quickly as appropriate.

Second Session - Broken Toy

During this session participants will watch a video – either a big screen for one showing to the whole body of participants or several smaller set-ups, one for each group.
The facilitator will also need a flipchart and paper and pens.

The video we recommend for this activity is "Broken Toy" made in America by Tom Brown. It has an activity book to accompany it and the package is suitable for young people aged eight years to about fourteen. A few other recordings are also suitable and are referenced in appendix 6. If an alternative is chosen then the activities must be modified.

Before showing the video give the students a list of points to watch for and display them on the flip chart for reference. They are:

* **Why is the clock important?**
* **Why is it called Broken Toy?**
* **What role do the girls play?**

Then watch the video - running time about 30 minutes.
Talk through the answers to the questions.

Importance of the clock:
Raymond is under threat all the time and the clock indicates the approach of break when he will be tormented in the play area.

The Broken Toy:
The bullies do not consider the feelings of their victim, regarding him as a toy. Discuss the difference between the phrases:
"I play with a toy" and "I play with a friend.".

The significance of the girls:
They were watchers who knew what was happening to Raymond but did nothing about it. After the accident they regret that they did nothing to intervene. Are they right to feel guilty?

Problem Solving
Set up small group discussions about how the teachers should have dealt with this situation. Provide sheets of paper and pens for the groups and ask them to devise a written action plan. Tell group members to record all their ideas, without discussion initially, and gradually to work out what the action plan would be.

The Class Action Plan
After the allotted time the facilitator should call the groups back together and take comments and suggestions from each small group. The ideas are recorded and discussed by the whole group. It may be possible to tease out some themes common to all plans.

The facilitator ends the session by explaining how bullying will be handled at this school and how important it is for the watchers or victims to tell. Ensure that time is allowed to close the session calmly and positively.

Afternoon Session - Choice of Workshops

Different workshop choices will allow all the students to select something they find interesting and enjoyable. The menu should include activities such as music, drama, dance, writing, poetry, art, model making.

If the choices are made before the day then staff will have time to organise suitable rooms and facilitators.

Drama

The best and most positive results are produced by the drama groups when they have been provided with outline notes for scenarios. Some examples are set out below.

> *Don't let others get involved!*
> A and B are good friends.
> C and D are known for their uninvited interference and are not particularly popular.
> A and B have an argument and walk off in a huff.
> A meets C and has a bit of a moan about B.
> C goes off and tells D that A has called B a slag etc. etc..... Really stirring it.
> A and B decide that they will make it up.
> D goes up to B and tells her what C has said, name calling etc. etc...
> B believes what has been said and says that she doesn't want to go round with A.
>
> Discussion points
> What is happening?
> How often has this happened to you?
> Who is in the wrong?
> How do we stop others getting involved and stop them from causing problems that do not exist?

> *I'll join in so that it doesn't happen to me.*
> A group of students are known to be unpleasant and another student joins the group. The new member tells the audience that she is only joining the group because if she doesn't the group will pick on her. The story can continue with the new member gradually changing the attitude and behaviour of the rest of the group and making them friendlier people.
>
> Discussion points
> Why is it difficult to change the behaviour of a group?

> *Why don't you tell?*
> A group are talking about a friend who is getting picked on. When the friend joins the group they ask why he is not telling anyone. Gradually they persuade the person to ask for help. They offer to go with him to tell a teacher, emphasising that they are helping others as well as themselves.
>
> Discussion points
> Why are young people reluctant to tell teachers about bullying?

> ***Re-run the opening sketches.***
> Remind the students of the opening scenarios from the introductory session [page 10] which illustrate different types of bullying. Plan and replay them with different endings to show how the situation could be handled better by the people involved.

Creative Writing

Facilitators can allow young people to write prose, poetry or drama generated from their own experiences, from events during the awareness day or from brainstorming group work. We have included some examples of poems children have written in appendix 5. The acrostic poems are very effective.

Dance

The success of this activity is very much in the hands of the dance teacher who should prepare the theme and the music. A suitable piece of music is The Jets and Sharks track from West Side Story. This encourages the students to show body language associated with bullying and the effects it can have on people.

Life-long bullying Bullying behaviour goes on throughout life and the group could be split up, demonstrating in movement, how babies demand attention, toddlers snatch toys, school and adult bullying. The dance can illustrate the power of the bully and the effects on the victim who suffers. Words, statements or rap can be added to complete the effect.

Art

Materials: quantities of magazines, felt pens, scissors, glue, paint, fabric, junk. Group efforts using collage technique will produce eye-catching and effective works of art in a very short time.
* Posters illustrating the rights of students
* Posters encouraging students that it is safe to tell
* Collages depicting the feelings of the people involved in bullying

Plenary

Following the afternoon sessions, we recommend that all the young people reconvene in the hall so that they can perform or present their work. If there is not time for each contribution to be taken, then ask for a few volunteers and explain that the others will be performed during future assemblies.

Finally the facilitator should review the aims of the day and take some comments from the participants. Remind the pupils that the day has been very important, the timetable was suspended and visitors have joined the school to support the work. Ask them to go home and talk about what they have learnt and achieved during the day.

The closing comments should state that when we watched the sketches in the morning we were all watchers and by watching and not doing anything about it we are colluders. We can help bullying to stop. Remind them of the last words in Broken Toy...

For someone
  * *to have a friend*
    * *to be simply left alone*
      * *to be accepted for what they are*
         would be like a dream

**And you can make those dreams come true.
It is everyone's responsibility to help stop bullying.**
Ξ

Plan for Model B

Groups of young people visit a series of activities in turn.

Like model A the day starts with the introduction described on pages 9 - 13. It is followed by a rotation through four or five different activities. Each group will take the programme in a different order so the activities are separate experiences which make up a full day.

A suggested and balanced menu might be chosen from:
    Art, Writing, Circle Time, Drama and Improvement Planning.

This variety ensures that all pupils are offered a range of different experiences.

For all the activities some suggestions are offered but facilitators will modify and develop the ideas. It is important that:
  * the activity offers a similar experience for each group and does not change significantly as the day progresses
  * that the facilitator is comfortable and confident with the plan.

Art Activities

Resources
Individual or group work
Variety of materials

Aim
To encourage pupils to think of visual ways to present strong, clear messages about bullying.

Introduction
Give a quick introduction picking up some of the points made during the first session. As the day progresses the young people will bring more ideas and experiences to the activity.

Format
Posters, simple graphics, cartoons or line drawings with caption or speech bubbles.

Ideas
How to stop bullying.
    This is a telling school
    A bully free area
    Bullying, it won't happen here
    Teasing hurts
    Don't just watch.... Do something to stop it.

What to do if you are bullied.
    Being bullied -tell somebody
    It's not smart to keep quiet

Pupils can work on their own or together to produce a series of linked posters or a joint effort. One school produced a wall of painted bricks on large sheets of paper. This made up into a graffiti wall on which students wrote contributions related to bullying.

Writing/Poetry

Resources
A variety of plain and decorative writing materials.
Word-processor and printer

Aim
    * to explore the feelings of people involved in bullying,
    * to create a set of guidelines regarding pupils' rights to feel safe in school

Introduction
Give a quick introduction picking up some of the points made during the first session. As the day progresses the young people will bring more ideas and experiences to the activity. Explain the purpose is to offer a better understanding of bullying as a social process.

Format
    * a story/poem about bullying
    * a classroom/school charter
    * a newspaper report about anti-bullying work in school

Ideas
Choose a reading from the selection in Appendix 5.
>That Long Road
>Sticks and Stones
>Acrostic Poems
>Bullies and Victims
>Classroom Charter
>Cats Eye
>A letter to a newspaper.

Some pupils might prefer to record their contributions on tape to be transcribed later. Pupils may work together if appropriate.

Circle Time Feelings
Arrange the chairs in a circle. The group leader is part of the "circle". Explain to the group that in this session they will discuss and explore the issue of bullying.

Explain the Rules
1. To allow everybody the opportunity to speak. Everybody will get an opportunity in turn to make a response.
2. Everybody may pass and say nothing.
3. Everyone must listen without comment to every contribution.
4. What is said in the group is confidential.

Role of the group leader
Encourage all contributions and make no disapproving comments. To put everyone at ease the first few activities are intended to relax the group.

My Name
Ask each student to check the name of the person seated to the right. Start by saying "My name is George and this is John" John then says,
>"My name is John and this is Mary."
>"My name is Mary and this is Jenny."

This process continues as each person says his or her own name and introduces the person on his or her right.

Silent Statements
This game will move the group out of their original seating arrangements and break up any groups of friends.
Explain you are going to make a statement, all those that conform to the statement stand up and change places with someone else who is standing up:
* all those who have a brother
* all those who have been to Spain
* all those who have seen people being bullied.

Now that bullying has been introduced you can move on to explore feelings about bullying. Some pupils might get upset in the following activities. Don't panic, acknowledge their feelings and give permission for an emotional response. Use an accepting phrase like,
>"Mary, I can see that this is upsetting you. It is quite normal for people to feel upset when we are discussing issues such as bullying".

This may be sufficient to allow the pupil to continue with the group activity. If the distress persists, give permission to leave the group, accompanied by another pupil. A support person should be available to stay with the upset pupil until s/he is ready to re-join the circle.

Guided Recall

Explain that a guided recall is an opportunity to remember some personal experiences of bullying. Most people find this easier if they close their eyes and sit in a relaxed position.

Read the three passages in a calm voice. Leave some time between them - do not rush on to the next statement. Allow time for reflection.

"Remember a time when you saw somebody being bullied. What happened? What did you do ? How did it make you feel ?"

"Remember a time when you were bullied, when people did something or said something that hurt you.
What did they say or do ? What did you do ? How did it make you feel ?"

"Remember a time when you did something unpleasant to another person.
What did you do ? Why did you do it ? How did it make you feel ?"

" I want you to come back from your memories."

Wait a little while, then give the next instruction.

Go round the circle asking for responses to some sentence completion activities:

* When I saw somebody being bullied I felt..............
* When I was bullied I felt.........
* When I did something unpleasant, I did it because.............., and I felt.............

Number the pupils into pairs

"Turn to the person next to you and discuss for three minutes how this school could reduce bullying, and how you could reduce bullying"

Go around the circle and ask each pair to state briefly what they discussed.

This should take most of your time. If you have time available ask the group to consider all of the suggestions made about reducing bullying and ask each individual to complete the statement

* The most important suggestion is................

Closing Activity

* Today I learned........

End the session and thank everybody for their participation.

Drama Group

Resources
Sticks and Stones Central TV programme [see pages 19 + 20 for other ideas].

Aim
To encourage pupils to think about:
* interpreting non-verbal behaviour
* why victims hide real feelings
* the importance of being "in" with the group.

To use role play to create empathy and to understand exclusion.

Introduction
Explain they are going to watch a video of a group of girls, there will be no sound track and they have to try to decide what is happening.

Format
A short section of video is used here showing a group of four teenage girls talking in a classroom [about 18 minutes into the programme]. Three of the girls are teasing the fourth. They make comments about her clothes and tease her about a party invitation.
The scene should be shown twice; once with the volume turned right down and again with the sound at normal volume.

After the first showing the group is asked to guess what is happening by observing body language only. After hearing the conversation the activity focuses on what intervention should be made to stop the bullying.

<u>Play video excerpt without sound</u>

Divide group into 4s. Ask them to decide what is happening. Allow about 3/4 minutes. [During this time rewind the video to the start of the excerpt and reset volume].

Take feedback and explore different ideas about what is happening. Ask for evidence for the interpretations.

<u>Play the same section of video with sound</u>

In the same groups ask the young people to discuss why the girl in the jumper doesn't walk away and why she doesn't tell the group how she is feeling.

Take feedback. Make the point that often when we are hurt we don't show our real feelings.

Ideas
Ask the groups to replay the scenes with the following variations:

> The girl off picture comes to the rescue and genuinely accepts the invitation to the party. The girl in the red jumper then follows suit and tells the girl in the black jumper to stop teasing.

> The group tease the victim, this time the victim stands up for herself, she tells them how hurtful their comments are.

Take feedback and watch a few "performances".

Discuss

How easy is it in real life to stand up for a victim when a group decides to be unpleasant towards one person?

How easy is it to stand up for yourself when a group picks on you? What would happen if you told the group how you were feeling.

Improvement Planning

Resources

Large sheets of paper and different coloured felt tip pens.

Aim

To look at:
* What schools can do to reduce bullying,
* What individuals can do to reduce bullying.

Introduction

Bullying occurs in every school. It is everybody's responsibility to reduce and stop bullying. Schools should be safe places for all pupils. Using your experiences from your life in schools, how could schools be safer places so that bullying is reduced?

Format

Ask the young people to draw upon their own experiences in schools and to think of lots of things schools can do to reduce bullying.

Set up small groups and give them some headings to work on:
- Before school starts
- In the classrooms
- Moving between lessons
- Toilets
- Breaks
- Lunch time
- After school
- Support for pupils

Allow about 12 minutes, and ask for responses written on the large sheets of paper using just one coloured felt tip.

Stop the activity.

Ask the groups to look at their lists and, by discussion, reach a consensus on the three most important ideas in order of priority. Underline these and number them in a different colour. Take some feedback.

Responsibility of the individual

In the last 15 minutes change the emphasis for responsibility from the organisation to the individual.

Say - "We all have a responsibility of making this a safe environment. What does this mean? What do we as individuals need to do ?"

Plenary Session

Welcome the whole group back together.

Ask them to talk, in pairs, to answer the questions:
* What have they learned?
* What had the biggest impact?

Take feedback.

Explain to the group that the purpose of the day has been to encourage every individual to understand what bullying is and to feel able to do something to help.

Replay the scenarios from the beginning of the day - giving each one a positive outcome:

* Someone intervenes and stops the bullying
* Some group members feel uncomfortable and refuse to join in
* The victim makes a clear statement about how hurt she feels
* A group member defines the behaviour as bullying and goes to a member of staff for help.

Make the following points. Use an OHP or a poster. Ξ

Bullying can happen to anyone.
> When it happens it is very upsetting.
> Victims feel very alone, miserable and sometimes desperate.
> Lots of nice young people join in and behave in a horrible way because it is fun; it makes them feel part of the group.
> Everyone should understand that nasty behaviour can be dreadfully hurtful.
> Everyone should feel powerful.
> Each one of you can do something positive.

Things you can do.
> Refuse to join in
> Tell the bullies to stop
> Be friendly to the victim
> Report the bullying to a teacher.

Sentence Completion

In pairs, ask the participants to finish the sentence,

> When I see someone being bullied I am going to.........

Close the session with an encouragement to make this a safe school.

Follow-up Work

Anti bullying work should be part of a continuous development within school, not just an annual event. Staff and student groups might explore such issues as:
* improving the environment
* curriculum content [especially P.S.E.]
* school or year group assemblies
* working party to monitor support structures
* development of successful, problem solving interventions
* involving parents - information and workshops
* peer mediation, buddy systems and support from older pupils.

A school publication

As a follow up, the school might wish to produce a booklet on bullying. Students could be involved in the production, including some of the art and creative work produced on the day. Signs for parents to look for in a child that is being bullied. A summary of the school policy should also be included.

The publication written for students by Andrew Mellor [1995] provides a positive starting point.

Appendices

1	Planning notes from one school	pages 29 - 30
2	Example of a letter to parents	page 31
3	Example of a student questionnaire	page 30
4	Evaluation formats and results	pages 33 - 35
5	Worksheets and overhead transparency sheets	
6	Bibliography and resources	

Appendix One - The Planning

These are real and un-edited notes from a school initiative.
The planning stage is very important and all staff must be kept informed. The following is how one school informed all staff of what was being planned. They were invited to future meetings and asked to contribute their ideas. Names have been removed, but other than this, this is the document that was circulated.

A day conference for the Noname School
Planners: a list of people involved.
Purpose of the conference:
To produce an enjoyable and memorable day through which all members of the community will increase their understanding, confidence and ability in handling people problems.

Outline of the day:
9 – 9.45 Introduction in Hall
GR Sets the scene
Role plays on stage
Pair work and other active involvement
9.50 – 10.35 Session 1
Each group to one activity
10.35 – 10.55 Break
Doughnuts from McDonald's(?) and pop, coffee for staff and visitors
10.55 – 11.40 Session 2
11.45 – 12.30 Session 3
12.30 – 1.15 Lunch
1.15 – 2.00 Session 4
2.05 – 2.50 Session 5
2.55 – 3.20 Conclusion in Hall
Results and role plays with a difference

Working out the Groups
Students will work in vertical groups [approximately 16 - 20] arranged within houses by the house heads. Advanced studies students may join in as adults or as students according to their preference.

Rolling programme of activities:
In each session every group of students will experience one of five activities. There will be approximately 9 groups undertaking the same activity at any one time.

The activities will be led by adult members of the school (including parents, governors, teachers, support staff, technicians, the administration team, and senior students), as far as possible according to their preference of activity. Each team leader will have a detailed brief to work from. The activities will be:

1. ART in as wide a range of media as possible (paint, collage, charcoal, clay...etc) leading to a wide range of visual interpretations (pictures, murals etc) of the experience of being involved in or associated with bullying. These could be presented at the end in some kind of **display.**

2. WRITING of different kinds to crystallise feelings and experiences, or to express basic rights. Some of the pieces could be collected and **published**.

3. CIRCLE ACTIVITIES. These activities include guided recall. They are designed to loosen people up and enable them to share in reflecting constructively on their experiences of bullying behaviour and the feelings involved.

4. DRAMA. This would involve studying videos of incidents and working out through small group drama alternative consequences.

5. IMPROVEMENT PLANNING. The group will identify steps which could be taken to make the school a place where bullying is less likely, including changes in the environment, in school organisation and in themselves. The approach would involve:
- **C** reative thinking
- **A** dult involvement
- **R** elating to other people
- **E** mpathy

Making it a special day

It will be a "no uniform" day, with "treats" at break for everyone. The school will show how important the day is by making it "high profile" with;
* well planned media involvement
* carefully prepared presentation to the students
* advance communication with parents.

Will it work?

There will be evaluation and follow-up as part of the University research programme, to see if there is an awareness of change and if the desired outcomes have occurred, including implementing the suggested improvements, and changes in attitude, feelings and behaviour.

Action Plan

1. Publicity - Media : Students: Parents' leaflet: Staff briefing
2. Student programmes
3. Refreshments – Doughnuts (and sponsorship?) from McDonald's, Coffee.
4. Student groupings.

Still to work out

The following list will be worked on at SMT meeting
Anyone interested and free will be welcome to come and join in.

1. Rooming in consultation with HFs
2. Budget
3. Staff groupings and other adults
4. Follow-up arrangements
5. Involvement of the Admin. Team
6. Group leaders' planning
7. Labels for everyone
8. How to manage the AGM
9. Arrangements for counselling if needed
10. Transport for AGM?
11. Managing the displays, presentations and displays, especially if they are to be around for the parents.

Appendix 2 - Letter to Parents

Dear Parents

At present there is much concern in this country about bullying, and the subject is a feature in many newspapers and magazines.

I know how anxious parents feel if their son or daughter is a victim of bullying or if they discover their child is bullying others.

Although teachers and those who work with young people discuss bullying, very little practical help has been given to young people who may have to cope with stressful situations. Fear of telling anyone and not knowing what to do can lead to much unhappiness at school and at home.

I want to emphasise that I don't think that there is any more bullying taking place in Newham School than anywhere else, but I do believe that our pupils should be as well prepared as possible to deal with it should it happen.

I am pleased to tell you that on Wednesday, 12th December a special training day has been arranged for pupils in years 8 and 9 when the theme will be bullying. The day will not be led by our own teachers but by a training team who are deeply concerned about the issues of bullying. The programme for the day will be very varied, and will not be serious! Discussions, a film, fun art work, drama and dance will be some of the possibilities.

In order to fit in the programme we are making some changes to the normal school day. Here they are:

1. No lessons!

2. The dinner break will be from 12.00 to 12.45. There will be school dinner at this earlier time. Please could all pupils bring a packed lunch or stay to school dinner that day, as the dinner break is short and a punctual start to the afternoon must be made at 12.45.

3. Tea or coffee and biscuits will be provided free for the morning break. The tuck shop will be open for any extras.

4. A cold drink will be made available for the afternoon break.

5. The afternoon will end at 2.45 as usual.

6. Pupils need not wear school dress but may come in casual clothes suitable for, say, drama or dance. Yes, jeans can be worn!

7. I have just been asked by the training team if a video may be made of the day. It would be used to help other schools and teachers. The video would not give the name of this school, and any pupils filmed would use assumed names. I hope that you will feel as I do that we should let our Training help as many other people as possible.

The training team and I hope that your daughter will enjoy next Wednesday very much.

Yours sincerely,

Headteacher
Newnham School

Appendix Three - Pupil Questionnaire [pre-event]

Name of school. [   ]

Are you a boy or a girl? [   ]   How old are you? [   ]

PLEASE TICK.

Have you been bullied in this school?   yes [ ]   no [ ]

How often has this happened?   once [ ]   twice [ ]   more [ ]

Were the bullies your age? [ ]   older than you [ ]   younger than you [ ]

Where did it happen?

in classroom [ ]   in toilets [ ]   in corridors [ ]

in playground [ ]   outside school [ ]   at home [ ]

If it happened somewhere not mentioned please describe the situation.

[   ]

Did you report it to a member of staff?   yes [ ]   no [ ]
Did you tell your parents?   yes [ ]   no [ ]
If you reported it, did this stop it?   yes [ ]   no [ ]
Have you seen other pupils being bullied?   yes [ ]   no [ ]
Did you report it?   yes [ ]   no [ ]

If you didn't report it can you please write down what stopped you.

[   ]

Should this school do more to stop bullying? yes [ ] no [ ]
If you have any ideas to help us stop bullying please write them down.

[   ]

If you would like to give your name so that a member of staff can talk to you about bullying please sign the form. We promise that this will be treated in confidence. Only sign this if you want to.   [   ]

Appendix Four - Evaluations

Group Leader Evaluation

Name   What group did you lead?

Was the preparation good, adequate, poor?

What else would have made the task easier?

What worked well for your group?

What did not work well?

Did you make any changes as the day progressed?
{detail}

How could the activity be improved for next time?

How did the students respond?

What did the students learn?

How well did the concluding session work?

Was the day a worthwhile use of time and resources? – comment please.

Thank you for your participation

Student Evaluation

We hope that you enjoyed our day together. We would like to hear some of your views about how the day went.

Please fill in this form and rely on your own opinions without talking to your friends.

How would you rate the parts of the day?
    Put a ring around the word that best describes your attitude.

Introductory talk	excellent	good	average	poor	awful
Art	excellent	good	average	poor	awful
Writing	excellent	good	average	poor	awful
Drama	excellent	good	average	poor	awful
Circle Time	excellent	good	average	poor	awful
The Environment	excellent	good	average	poor	awful
Closing talk	excellent	good	average	poor	awful

What was the best part of the day?

What made it so good?

What was the worst part of the day?

What made it so bad?

What did you learn?

How will you change your behaviour:
    If you are bullied?

How will you change your behaviour:
    If you see it happening?

Thank you for your participation

Results of Pupil Evaluation

Three hundred and fifty replies were received in time for inclusion in the analysis below. The table represents percentage responses.

	Excellent	Good	Average	Poor	Awful
Introductory Talk	24	58	17	0.5	0.5
Art	25	45	23	6	1
Writing	16	45	32	5	2
Drama	39	34	21	4	2
Circle Time	32	42	17	6	3
The Environment	9	50	32	8	1
Closing Talk	26	50	20	2	1
Total = the day as a whole	24	46	23	4.5	1.5

70% of students thought the day was good or excellent
23% of students thought the day was average
6% of students thought the day was poor or worse

Words used to describe the day included:
Interesting, fun, enjoyable, relaxed, clear and entertaining, amusing but serious, George Robinson knew what he was talking about.

Positive aspects of the day:
The doughnuts, no uniform, being able to share, being able to express ourselves, people were nice to each other, all the different activities, sharing experiences, the presence of the media, being able to say what you think, writing poems, drama, teachers had fun but could be serious too, the circle time and being able to talk in a group, being on radio, being on TV., doing posters, watching videos, having our photos taken.

Negative aspects:
It went on too long, too much talking, the hall got hot, boring, repetition.

What was learned:
To talk to someone if you have problems, what forms bullying takes, how the victim feels, to help others with problems, how to cope with bullying, bullies have problems too.

The points they noted apart from the content included:
the doughnuts (the school provided doughnuts for all pupils), no uniforms, the presence of the media, being on radio, being on TV., having our photos taken, (the school had a parent who was a photographer to take photographs, that were later used to make a display).

It really helps the pupils to remember the day if you make it special.

See pages 36 onwards:
Appendix Five - Worksheets and overhead projection sheets

Sticks and Stones

I can remember sitting on top of this shed with Jane and Emma. We were hidden from the path by the trees and bushes. Katy walked by and we started to call her names, really nasty things about the way she looked and dressed. She was angry and yelled back at us, "Sticks and stones will break my bones but names will never hurt me!".... so we started to throw sticks and stones at her.

Looking back on it I can hardly believe that I did that. I was always nice to Katy. Her mother had died and she lived alone with her father who was quite old and he used to get her really unfashionable clothes. I felt sorry for her and I spent a lot of time looking out for her when other kids were unkind. Even so, on that day when I was hidden away with my best friends, I joined in without even thinking about how Katy must have felt. We laughed at the time.

Now I cringe at what I did when I was ten.

Twenty-one year old student.

That Long Road

Walking up that road to school
I consider turning back.
I consider running to that special point,
my own special point.
I consider going to their houses
And telling their Mums.
I consider ruining their lives somehow,
to make them feel scared.
Then suddenly I am in school,
they take my bag, ruffle my hair.
Maybe some other day.

by Kate Hartoch

BULLYING - an acrostic poem

Being all by myself
Useless as can be
Living in a world of fear
Left out of all the fun
Yearning for some company
I wish I could find
New friends to make me happy
Going out of my mind.

Bullies and Victims.

Victim speaks:

I stand in the shadows at playtime
Observing the popular crowd.
They've just teased me yet again
Made me ashamed, standing with my head bowed.
"You should have a better sense of humour," they say.
"We all know that you don't mind."
But is that your guilt saying that
as you know you're being unkind?

Bully speaks:

I catch her eye, standing over there
and feel sorry I said all that stuff
but they all laughed, with me, at her.
Why do you think we are so tough?
I feel sorry for her, though I never say that.
And always a friend she's hoping to find.
But she's right you know, about one thing
I'm guilty of being unkind.

With thanks to Becky aged 13.
Brahma Kumaris Spiritual University 22/5/93

Fun for one may be pain for another

All the kids in the class think it's fun to call Mary and Tom names because they wear glasses. They call them Speccies, Four Eyes, Cow and Gate, Goggle Eyes etc.

It has no effect on Tom, he feels good in his glasses, he has designer frames and everybody in his family wears glasses. He laughs it off.

For Mary, it is different. The family is short of money and she couldn't get the fashionable designer frame glasses she wanted. She got the cheapest frames in the shop. Nobody else in her family wears glasses, she pretends she doesn't care, but deep down she's desperate for the name calling to stop. It's killing her!

Aims for the day

to agree that bullying happens

to agree that bullying is damaging to the person that receives it

to agree that bullies are not nasty people and may not be fully aware of how their behaviour damages other people

to extend the definition of bullying to a wider range of behaviours

to learn something about group process

to experience group work

to provide opportunity through creative work for young people to express feelings about bullying

to provide empowering opportunities for problem solving "what can we do", "what will we do"

to celebrate the work done on the day

to prepare for further work to be done in the future

A School Classroom Covenant.

I have a right
- to be treated with respect and kindness. This means that nobody will laugh at me, ignore me, or hurt my feelings.

I have a right
- to be an individual in this room. This means that nobody will treat me unfairly because of my interests, or that I'm boy or girl, fat or thin, fast or slow.

I have a right
- to be safe in this room. This means no-one will hit me, kick me, push me, taunt me with words or hurt me in any way.

I have a right
- to learn about myself in this room. This means I will be free to express my feelings and opinions without fear of being interrupted or punished.

I have a right
- to be valued and respected for my individual strengths and weaknesses.

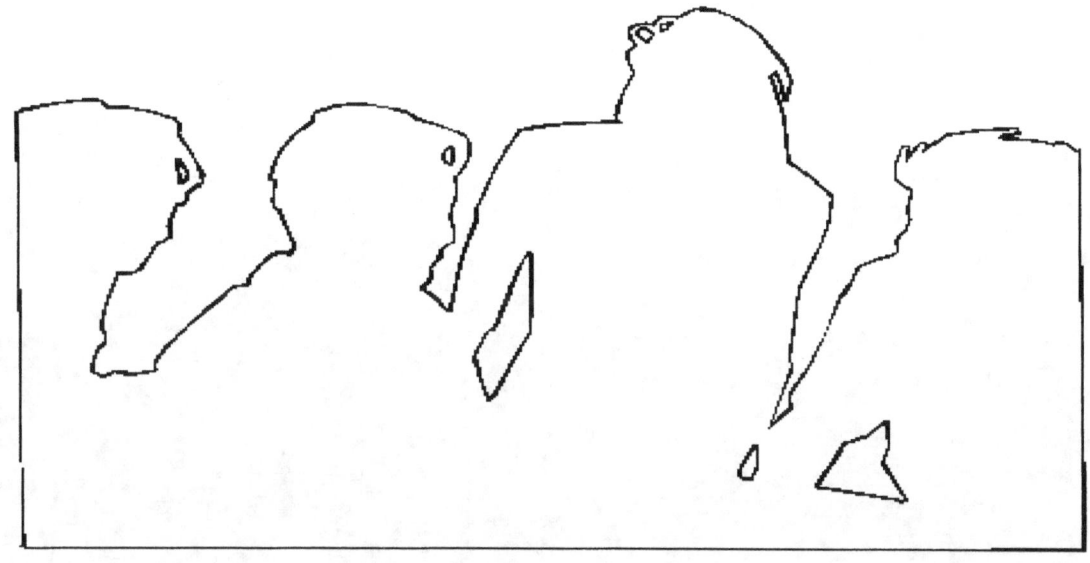

Bullying can happen to anyone.
When it happens it is very upsetting.
Victims feel very alone, miserable and sometimes desperate.
Lots of nice young people join in and behave in a horrible way because it is fun; it makes them feel part of the group.
Everyone should understand that nasty behaviour can be dreadfully hurtful.
Everyone should feel powerful.
Each one of you can do something positive.

Things you can do.
Refuse to join in
Tell the bullies to stop
Be friendly to the victim
Report the bullying to a teacher.

"Victims have no friends."

Before taking his life the boy wrote a message in the class diary, a portion of which I quote.

"I decided to kill myself because day after day I go to school and only bad things happen. Nothing good ever happens to me. If the kids in my class could be in my shoes they would understand how I feel. If only they knew how I feel every day. Even in my dreams there are nothing but bad things.

The only one I can talk to is the hamster, but the hamster can't speak back. Maybe my being born was a mistake... I can't stop the tears now. There was one, only one thing I wanted while I was alive, a friend I could talk to, really talk to from the heart. Just one friend like that, only one, was all I wanted."

Picking on Someone

Jack Straw, the MP, wrote this which clearly describes how a group of children decided to pick on somebody who they made different.

"It wasn't classical bullying. There was no single big lad beating up a smaller one. Indeed very little of the bullying was physical at all. It was verbal, psychological, insidious and, in many ways the worse for that.

Paul had been chosen as the odd one out. I have no idea how the rest of us made that choice. Certainly it was never a conscious decision. But the rest of us - each of whom, I guess, also found the frugal atmosphere of a Fifties boarding school quite hard to bear - picked on Paul. He smelt - but didn't we all with only one bath and one clean shirt a week, who wouldn't? He was stupid - though his academic results were the same as the rest of us. He didn't join in. We made sure of that.

Above all he was different. I can't for the life of me remember why, or how, except that we had to make him different and we did."

Jack Straw - Daily Mirror. January 18th 1995

Victims have no backbone!

"You have to learn how to stand up for yourself," says my mother. "Don't let them push you around. Don't be spineless. You have to have more backbone."

I think of sardines and their backbones. You can eat their backbones. The bones crumble between your teeth in one touch and they fall apart. This must be what my own backbone is like; hardly there at all. What is happening to me is my own fault, for not having more backbone.

CATS EYE
Margaret Attwood (1990).

Broken Toy

For someone
* to have a friend
* to be simply left alone
* to be accepted for what they are

would be like a dream

And you can make those dreams come true.

It is everyone's responsibility to help stop bullying.

Letter to the Editor

Cruel Bullies

have driven my friends from school.

Two of my friends are too scared to come to school because of verbal bullying. The teachers don't seem to know what to do. My friends told the teachers a few weeks ago and they told the bullies to stop and gave them a detention. This seems to have made the bullying worse.

The teachers also told my friends to ignore the teasing and name calling but that hasn't worked. I know how terrible it is to be bullied like this because it happened to me last term.

The kids who are doing this think it's really funny. I don't but I don't know what to do.

Stephanie aged 14

Editor's reply.
Dear Stephanie

Bibliography.

ATTWOOD, M. (1990) Cats Eye. London, Virago Press.

BESAG, V. (1989) Bullies and victims in school. Milton Keynes, Open University Press.

D.F.E. (1994) Bullying, Don't suffer in silence. London, H.M.S.O.

MAINES, B & ROBINSON, G. (1991) Stamp out bullying. Lucky Duck Publishing.

ROBINSON, G. & MAINES, B. (1994) If it makes a my life easier to write a policy on BULLYING. Lucky Duck Publishing.

STRAW, J. (1995) Burdened by memories of bullying. Daily Mirror. 18.1.1995.

YOSHIO, M. (1985) Bullies in the Classroom. Japan Quarterly. Vol. 32, pages 407- 411.

BLISS, T. & TETLEY, J. (1993) Circle Time. Lucky Duck Publishing.

BLISS, T, ROBINSON, G & MAINES, B. (1995) Developing Circle Time. Lucky Duck Publishing.

BLISS, T, ROBINSON, G & MAINES, B. (1995) Coming Round to Circle Time. Lucky Duck Publishing. (video)

BROWN, T. ROBINSON, G & MAINES, B.(1993) Broken Toy. Lucky Duck Publishing.(video)

CENTRAL TELEVISION. Sticks and Stones. Broad Street, Birmingham. (video)

MAINES, B. & ROBINSON. G. (1991) Stamp out Bullying. Lucky Duck Publishing.(Video.)

MAINES, B. & ROBINSON. G. (1992) Michaels's Story, The No Blame Approach. Lucky Duck Publishing.(video)

MELLOR, A. (1995) Stopping Bullying. Lucky Duck Publishing. (a leaflet for young people in School.)

www.ingramcontent.com/pod-product-compliance
Lightning Source LLC
Chambersburg PA
CBHW050716090526
44587CB00019B/3400